MAY   2015

Sarika

THE SUN
A Super Star

by Chaya Glaser

Consultant: Karly M. Pitman, PhD
Planetary Science Institute
Tucson, Arizona

BEARPORT
PUBLISHING

New York, New York

Credits
Cover, © Triff/Shutterstock; TOC, © NASA/SDO (AIA); 4–5, © Triff/Shutterstock;
6–7, © Wikipedia & NASA; 8–9, © Wikipedia & NASA; 10, © Surachet Meewaew/
Shutterstock; 11, © NASA/NOAA/GSFC/Suomi NPP/VIIRS/Norman Kuring; 12, © NASA/
NOAA/GSFC/Suomi NPP/VIIRS/Norman Kuring; 13, © Lakov Kalinin/Shutterstock;
14–15, © Triff/Shutterstock; 16–17, © Associated Press; 18–19, © NASA/ESA; 20, © NASA/
SDO (AIA); 21, © Imagesource/Glow; 23TL, © oksix/Shutterstock; 23TM, © iStock/
Thinkstock; 23TR, © Wikipedia & NASA; 23BL, © NASA/ESA; 23BM, © NASA/SDO (AIA);
23BR, © Associated Press.

Publisher: Kenn Goin
Editor: Jessica Rudolph
Creative Director: Spencer Brinker
Design: Deborah Kaiser
Photo Researcher: Michael Win

Library of Congress Cataloging-in-Publication Data

Glaser, Chaya, author.
    The sun : a super star / by Chaya Glaser.
        pages cm. — (Out of this world)
    Includes bibliographical references and index.
    ISBN 978-1-62724-569-2 (library binding) — ISBN 1-62724-569-3 (library binding)
    1. Sun—Juvenile literature. I. Title.
    QB521.5.G53 2015
    523.7—dc23
                                2014036487

For more information, write to Bearport Publishing Company, Inc., 45 West 21st Street, Suite 3B,
New York, New York 10010. Printed in the United States of America.

10 9 8 7 6 5 4 3 2 1

CONTENTS

What object is the center of Earth's Solar System?

THE SUN!

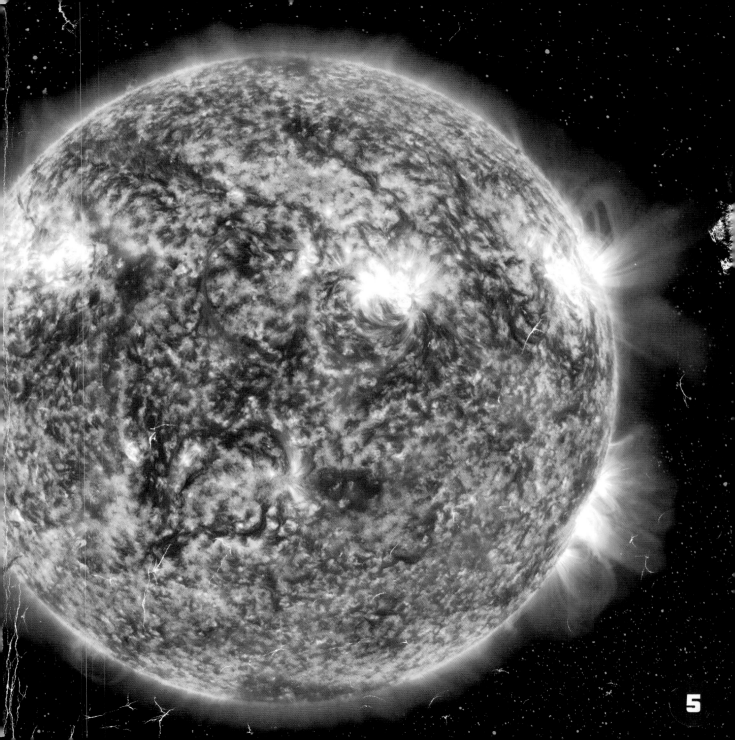

Eight planets orbit, or move around, the Sun.

SUN

MERCURY

VENUS

EARTH

MARS

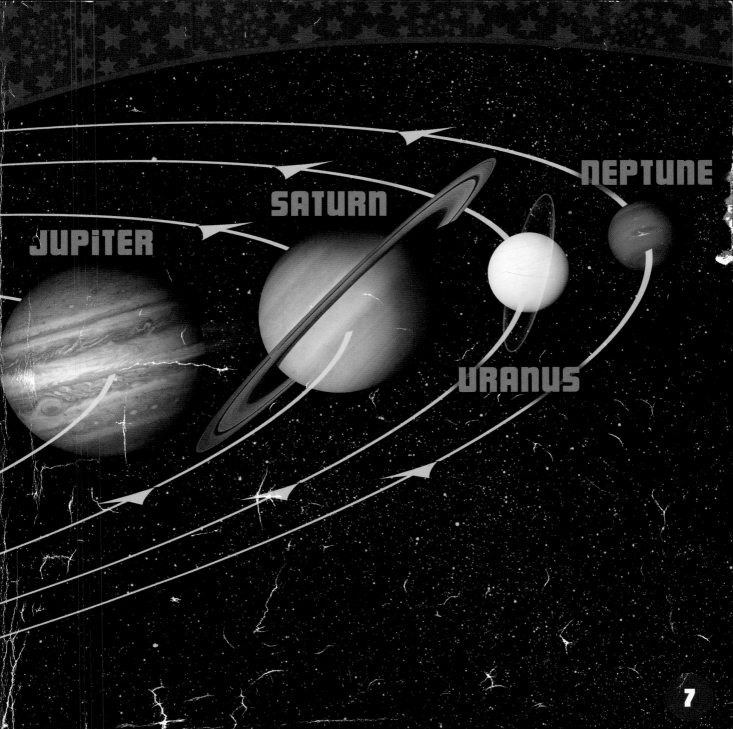

JUPITER

SATURN

NEPTUNE

URANUS

The Sun is a star.

It is the closest star to Earth.

MERCURY

VENUS

EARTH

The Sun is 93 million miles
(150 million km) from Earth.

We don't see the Sun at night like the other stars.

WHY?

Earth is always spinning.

Nighttime

EARTH

SUN

At night, part of Earth faces away from the Sun.

In the daytime,
part of Earth faces
the Sun.

SUN

Daytime

EARTH

This is when we see the Sun's bright light.

The Sun is the largest
object in our Solar System.

It is so large that more than one million Earths could fit inside it!

Earth

The Sun is made of gases and energy.

Its surface is a super-hot 9,939°F (5,504°C)!

Layers of gases and energy

Sometimes, gases and energy shoot out from the Sun's surface.

This is called a **solar flare**.

sun

19

The Sun gives us light and heat.

EARTH

SUN

It gives plants energy to grow.

People, plants, and animals could not live without the Sun!

SUN VERSUS EARTH

SUN	VERSUS	EARTH
Center of the Solar System	POSITION	93 million miles (150 million km) away from the Sun
864,337 miles (1,391,016 km) across	SIZE	7,918 miles (12,743 km) across
About 9,939°F (5,504°C)	AVERAGE TEMPERATURE	59°F (15°C)
Gases and energy	SURFACE	Mostly water, some land

GLOSSARY

energy (EN-ur-jee) the power needed by all living things to grow, develop, and stay alive

gases (GASS-iz) substances that float in the air and are neither liquid nor solid; many gases are invisible

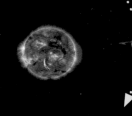

orbit (OR-bit) to circle around a planet, the Sun, or another object

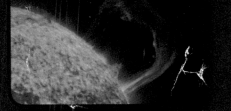

solar flare (SOH-lur FLAIR) a flash of brightness above the Sun in which energy is released

Solar System (SOH-lur SISS-tuhm) the Sun and everything that circles around it, including the eight planets

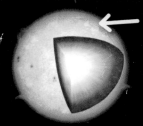

surface (SUR-fiss) the top layer of something

INDEX

READ MORE

Chrismer, Melanie. *The Sun (Scholastic News Nonfiction Readers).* New York: Children's Press (2005).

Lawrence, Ellen. *The Sun: The Star of Our Solar System (Zoom Into Space).* New York: Ruby Tuesday Books (2014).

LEARN MORE ONLINE

To learn more about the Sun, visit
www.bearportpublishing.com/OutOfThisWorld

ABOUT THE AUTHOR

Chaya Glaser enjoys looking up at the stars and reading stories about the constellations. When she's not admiring the night sky, she can be found playing musical instruments.